TIMEWARP™

Rome
anthology

TABLE OF CONTENTS

A Place Called Rome

Climb aboard, my fair friend.
We'll travel far away from home
To a place of adventures that never end.
We'll go to a place called Rome.

We'll walk together down ancient paths,
Witness great chariot races,
Spend lazy afternoons at the Roman baths,
And see many other wonderful places.

As we travel the land, we will hear,
Of great rulers and mighty Roman soldiers,
Who filled the hearts of their enemies with fear,
Carrying the life of an empire on their shoulders.

As time wears on, we'll stop to dine,
On tasty meats, sauces, and stuffed dates.
We'll be entertained and treated most fine,
As we taste of the foods on our plates.

We'll rise up and go on to admire
How the Romans worked, believed, and played.
We'll get to know this great empire
And the mark on the world it made.

When from this land we have returned
And come once more to our home,
Much it is we will have learned
From this ancient place called Rome.

THE ROMANS

People who come from the city of Rome are called Romans. Rome is in Italy. It began thousands of years ago. It became a great empire in the world. It began with some villages near the Tiber River. They stood on seven hills. One was Palatine Hill. The villages joined. They formed a town.

Kings ruled the land for 400 years. One of the last kings had twin grandsons. The king was overthrown. His grandsons were left to die at Palatine Hill. It was said that a wolf found them. It cared for them. They grew strong. They founded the city of Rome where they had been left to die.

Time passed. The Romans took over other lands. They made the lands part of the empire. Kings ruled first. Then, men called senators were in charge. The last rulers were emperors.

There were three groups of people in Rome. There were citizens. They were men. Some were rich. They could help rule as senators. Some were businessmen. Others were common men. The citizens could vote. The second group was women and children. They could not vote. Slaves were the third group. Citizens owned them. They had to work hard for no pay. Many were treated badly. Most came from lands the Romans took over.

Romans spoke Latin. Many English words came from Latin. *Language* came from *lingua*. *Lingua* is a Latin word. It means "tongue."

The letters B.C. and A.D. tell about Roman dates. B.C. means "before Christ." A.D. stands for Anno Domini. It means "in the year of Christ." The Roman Empire was strongest in 100 A.D. It had 60 million people.

Researchers dug to find remains of the empire. The digging, or excavating, was how people learned about the Romans. They learned much about how the Romans lived from the things they found.

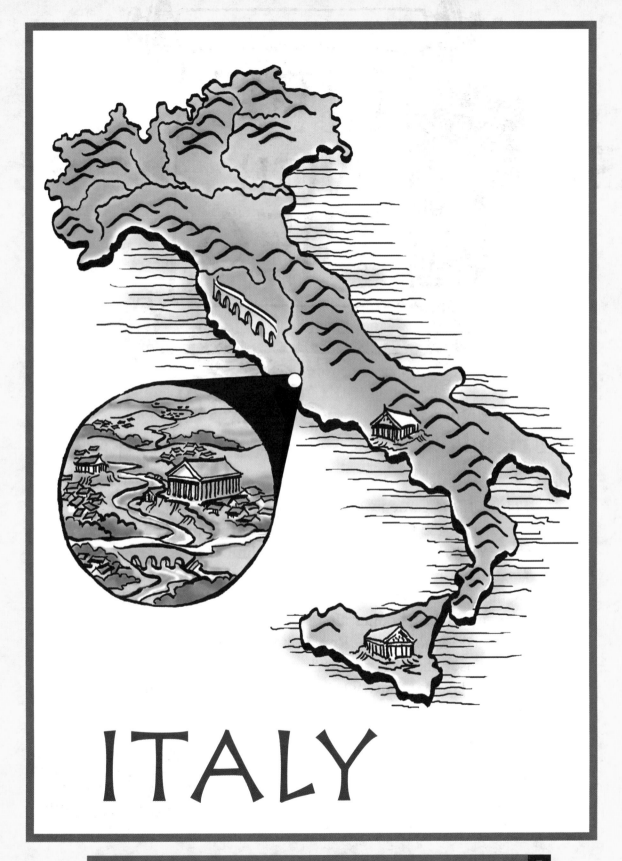

ITALY

Chapter One:
Friends

Plop! Off the garden wall she jumps. *Pitter. Patter. Pitter. Patter.* Across the rows of roof tiles she steps. *Scritch. Scratch. Scritch. Scratch.* Down the fig tree she climbs.

Tip. Tap. Tip. Tap. She trots through a room. The room has a shiny marble floor. Into the warm kitchen she proudly walks. It's the end of the day after all.

Meet Theo. She is a tiny Roman kitten. She lives in a Roman house. She lives with her family. The house is far from the city. Today in the city was busy. Now she is home for the night. Theo has the house all to herself while her family sleeps.

Sniff. Sniff. Theo's nose tells her that her family ate fish for dinner. She rushes to the special clay bowl. It has her name on it. The little girl in the house made it just for Theo. Theo finds a fish inside the bowl.

First, she eats until the bowl is empty. Theo is quite full. Next, she stretches and yawns near the warm fireplace. Last, she crawls to the top of the soft flour sack. The flour

inside is used to make bread. Theo thinks it is her bed. She tries to take a little catnap. After all, Theo is such a little kitten. It's the end of a very busy day.

Theo dreams about the day with her friend. The friend gives Theo a ride on her back around the racetrack. Then, they play a game of hide-and-seek in the hay. It is easy for Theo to hide. It is hard for the friend to find her. After all, she is such a small kitten. The friend is quite a large horse. The two friends have a treat when the fun and games end.

Squeak. Squeak. Theo hears a noise coming from the corner of the kitchen. She opens one eye ever so slowly. A mouse scampers across the floor. Theo quickly jumps up. After the mouse Theo goes. *Whoosh*! Out the kitchen door and across the shiny marble floor the mouse runs. Theo is close behind it. Theo's job is chasing mice in her house. The father says so.

The mouse gets lost in the garden outside. That does not bother Theo. The fish in the pond are much more interesting. The fish love to tease Theo. They swim to the top of the pond. She listens. *Blup. Blup. Blup.* They are talking to her. She watches them. *Swish. Swish.* Her tail moves back and forth all the while. Theo does not want to catch those fish. They are not hers. They are the boy's pet fish.

Back in the garden, Theo leaps at the moths and fireflies. She sees the vegetable. Theo knows just what to do. She digs and digs. Digging is a great chore. She works hard. She gets tired. Then, she finally finishes. She hides the vegetable behind the fig tree.

Now Theo is hungry once again. She sits among the grapevines. She helps herself to the grapes. *Gulp. Gulp.* The grapes are ripe and plump. She eats one after another. Theo curls up into a tiny fur ball. She takes a catnap on the moonlit night. Theo is a wee kitten after all and very full.

As the sun rises, so does Theo. *Sniff. Sniff.* She races into the kitchen. She smells her family's breakfast. She leaps onto the table. She licks the warm cakes dripping with honey. Theo laps goat's milk from the urn. *Slurp. Slurp.* It is a perfect breakfast for a Roman kitten. She gives herself a bath in front of the fireplace. Theo must prepare for the busy day ahead.

Theo knows it is time to start her day. She hears her family stirring. So . . .

Out of the kitchen she goes. *Tip. Tap. Tip. Tap.* Across the shiny marble floor she trots. *Scritch. Scratch. Scritch. Scratch.* Up the fig tree she climbs with the vegetable in her mouth. *Pitter. Patter. Pitter. Patter.* Across the rows of roof tiles she steps. *Plop.* Down she jumps onto the garden wall. Into the city she proudly walks with a gift for her friend. It's a new day after all.

Chapter Two:
At the Baths

It is a fine morning. The mother and little girl are going to the city. Theo watches. She wants to follow. She is curious. Down the stone path the mother and the little girl walk. They do not know Theo is following. She is a quiet and clever kitten after all.

There is a building in the city. It has many rooms. The mother and little girl go inside. Theo sneaks in the building behind them. They do not know she is there. Water from the spout flows into the pool. Some people are talking and laughing. Others are reading. Some are eating. Many are bathing. She gets out of sight of the mother and little girl. Theo gets lost in the bathhouse.

She pitters and patters into a room with children. They are playing a game. The game uses small colored glass balls. Theo wants to play too. She waits and watches. A bright blue ball rolls past Theo. She bats it with her paws.

Out of one room and into another goes Theo. She chases the rolling ball. People are reading and talking. No one else sees Theo. The ball rolls behind a tall pot on the floor. Theo thinks the pot would be a good place to climb. It has lovely designs and two large handles.

Theo jumps again and again. She finally grabs onto one handle of the pot using her paws. She climbs the side of the pot. Theo reaches the top by lifting herself up.

She pitters and patters around the rim of the pot. Theo is feeling quite proud of herself by now. She does not notice the slippery rim. Theo falls into the pot with a bloop!

Out of the pot she leaps. Poor Theo is covered with oil. The sweet smelling oil is used for bathing. She races into the next room. She is dripping puddles of oil. Theo slips and slides on the warm tiled floor.

She skids to a stop at the edge of a huge pool. People are having fun. A roly-poly woman jumps into the pool. Everyone gets splashed with water. Theo gets splashed the most. The poor kitten is frightened. She is oily. Most of all she is wet. People are laughing because Theo looks so very odd.

Theo feels something soft and warm. It surrounds Theo and lifts her up high. It is the little girl. Down the stone road they walk. Theo, the little girl, and the mother are going home to their house, far from the city.

In the cozy kitchen Theo laps a bowl of warm goat's milk. The little girl gently rubs her until the oil is gone. Theo curls up by the fire to dry. She purrs softly. She is happy to be home. After all, it has been a busy morning at the baths.

Chapter Three:
Off to School

Today is the day the boy goes to school. The boy has a soft bag. The bag carries all of his school things. The boy places a wax tablet inside the bag. The boy places a long writing tool inside the bag. He will use the tool to write his lessons on the tablet. Theo waits and watches.

The boy thinks about something as he walks across the tiled floor. He needs the meal he will take to school. Theo waits and watches. The boy sets the bag down. He packs a meal while in the kitchen. He packs bread. He packs cheese. He packs a fig, too. Theo climbs into the soft bag. She waits and listens. The boy places his meal inside the bag. He does not see Theo.

He picks up his heavy bag. He walks to the school in the city. Theo likes the cheese inside the bag. After all, she is a hungry kitten. The boy arrives at school. He sets the bag on the floor. He begins his day at school. He counts beads and reads numbers.

Theo quietly climbs out of the bag. She hides under a large scroll on the floor. Theo waits and watches. It is time for the boy to write his lesson on the wax tablet. The teacher says he must write his lesson again. He scrapes away the letters. He uses the other end of the long writing tool. He writes the same lesson again and again. Theo waits and watches.

The lesson is finished after many hours. The boy is glad. He has written the same lesson three times. He is ready for a meal. The finished lesson is set aside. The boy takes his food out of the soft bag. He looks for his cheese. It is not there. Maybe he forgot to pack the cheese. Theo waits and watches. The boy and his teacher go outside to eat in the sunshine. Out comes Theo from under the scroll.

Theo has been watching. She wants to write, too. First, she licks the wax tablet. It does not taste good. Next, she steps across the tablet. She leaves paw prints in the wax. Theo does not like the way the wax feels on the pads of her feet. Last, she decides to sharpen her claws on it. Her claws cut into the wax deeply. The boy and his teacher return. Theo runs and hides beneath the scroll on the floor. She waits and watches.

The boy is surprised when he sees the wax tablet. He looks around the room. He spies Theo hiding. Into the bag go Theo and the wax tablet. The boy must repeat his lesson tomorrow. The teacher tells Theo she is not yet ready for school.

Romulus and Remus:
The Founders of Rome

Long ago, there lived a king. His name was Numitor. He and his people lived in the hills near the Tiber River. The kingdom was called Alba.

Numitor was not a warrior. Armies did not matter to him. He was kind. He was gentle. He was good. He wanted people to live well and in peace.

The king had a brother. His name was Antony. He hated the king. He was jealous of him.

One day, Antony called his army. They attacked the king's home. They did not kill him. They knew the people loved the king. The people would have been too angry with the army if they had killed him.

Numitor was sent away from his home. His daughter, the princess, was put in prison so she could never marry. Antony did not want her to have a son who might one day be king.

Antony took the throne. He made himself king. He began to rule. He was not kind. He was not gentle. The people did not love him. They feared his army.

Time passed. The princess escaped from prison. She fled to another kingdom. She lived quietly there. After some years, she had twin sons. Her husband did not like babies. He made her take them away.

The princess took the babies to the Tiber River. "What can I do, my sweet twins? Your father cares not for you. I will leave you here. Someone may find you. She will show you mercy. Know that your mother loves you." With a heavy heart, she laid them on her robe. She left them on the riverbank.

Soon, a wolf found the babies. They lay on the robe. They were crying. The wolf sniffed the robe. She picked up the robe and the babies. She carried them to her den.

The babies lived with the wolf. She nursed them until they could eat. One day she went looking for food. The farmer Aspar came upon the den. He heard cries. They were not wolf pups. He went closer. He looked inside the den. He saw the twins. He took them home.

Aspar's wife was overjoyed. She loved babies. Then, she saw the robe. "Husband, do you not know what this is?" she asked.

The farmer replied. "It's just a robe."

"It's not just a robe," his wife responded. "The robe bears royal marks. It must belong to the daughter of Numitor. I heard women at the market talking. They said she escaped from prison. She married. She had twins. Her husband made her take them away. Soon after, she died of a broken heart."

"What will we do?" the man asked.

"We will rear them as our own," his wife said. "They have nowhere to go. Numitor is gone. He cannot help them. Their father does not want them. The new king will want to kill them."

"It will be as you say," said Aspar. "No one must know who they are. We will keep them safe. We will call them Romulus and Remus."

The boys grew. They were fast and light on their feet. Romulus was bigger. Remus was handsome. Romulus was thoughtful. Remus was quick to act.

The twins worked hard. Romulus tilled the land. Remus tended sheep. After work, Romulus made things. He carved figures from wood. He made shapes from clay. Remus liked the woods. He ran and hunted with wolves.

One day while tending sheep, Remus grew sleepy. He sat down by a tree. He took a nap. Soon, he was shaken awake. He looked up to find two big men standing over him. They took him away with them.

While Remus napped, the sheep had wandered onto his neighbor's land—again. Remus did not know that his neighbor was none other than his real grandfather, Numitor. The men took him to Numitor.

When he saw Remus, the king asked, "Who stands before me?"

"King, this boy slept by a tree while his sheep ate your crops," said one of the men. "What should we do with him?"

The king looked at Remus. He looked in the boy's eyes. He felt as if he had looked into them before. A thought came to him. It couldn't be! His voice trembled as he spoke. "Who are you?" he asked.

"I am Remus," replied the boy. "I'm sorry for the harm to your crops."

The king was silent. He asked, "Who are you really, boy?"

Remus did not know what to think. "I told you, sir," he said. "I am Remus."

At that moment, there was a cry at the door. "Please let us in! The boy meant no harm! Please!" It was Aspar. Romulus had heard his brother cry as the men took him. He went to find the farmer. They hoped to save Remus from a bad fate.

"Let them in," said the king.

His men opened the door. Romulus and Aspar entered. "Who are you?" asked the king. His eyes met Romulus's. His heart began to pound. Something was odd about this young man, too.

"I am Aspar. This is Romulus. He is Remus's twin brother. Please forgive my boy. I know he has been careless." The king did not speak. Aspar went on, "Remus tries to be good. I'm sure he will tend the sheep more closely now."

The king looked from Romulus to Remus and back again. "Are the boys your sons?" he asked.

The farmer did not know what to think. He said, "Yes, they are. I have cared for them as my sons for most of their lives."

"Go on," said Numitor. "Tell me everything about them."

Aspar felt nervous. He looked at the king's men. He and the boys were no match for them. "Bring water," Numitor told the men. The men went away. The king said, "I don't care about the crops. They will grow again. I want to know who your sons are. I must know. Tell me. How did they come to you?"

Aspar felt he must tell. He told how he came upon the wolf's den. He told how he heard crying. When he spoke of the robe, King Numitor stood. A pained look was on his face.

"The robe," he said, "how did it look?"

"It was fine, but dirty. It was white satin. The trim was purple like the clothes of a wealthy person. Silver leaves were stitched at the edges," said Aspar.

Numitor slumped in his chair. He put his hands to his face. He began to weep. Aspar was afraid. "Neighbor, I am sorry. I tell the truth. Have I said something to hurt you?"

The king's men had returned with the water. One spoke to Aspar. "Do you still have the robe?"

"Yes, my wife would not get rid of it," Aspar answered. "She thought it belonged to a princess. She heard women tell of King Numitor's daughter. They told how she escaped from prison. They said she married and had twins. Her husband made her abandon them. Then, she died of a broken heart. My wife and I kept the babies safe. King Antony would kill them. He could not know about them."

Numitor said, "Bring the robe. I must see it."

"Go, Romulus," said Aspar. As the door shut, Aspar spoke again. "I know you as the man who owns the land next to mine. I must ask. Who are you?"

The king's men stepped close to Aspar. Numitor held up his hand. They stopped. He spoke, "I am Numitor. The story the women told your wife is of my daughter. The boys you have reared as your sons are my grandsons. I am sure the robe will prove it. I have longed to know my daughter's fate. Now I know. She is dead. Yet, she lives. I see her in the eyes of Romulus and Remus."

Anger crossed Numitor's face. "Antony has caused much sadness and loss. I lost my kingdom. I lost my family. My child lost her children. She even lost her life. The people suffer every day under his rule. All must be made right."

Romulus returned with the robe. The king saw it. He began to cry again. He clutched it. Then, he embraced his grandsons. The boys did not know what to do. Aspar was their father. Now, he stood back.

Aspar and the twins dined with the king. The king spoke of life in Alba before Antony. They listened. The twins grew angry. They thought of all that had been lost. It had been taken from them. They left the king's home with thoughts of putting matters back in order.

Time passed. The twins grew older. They became stronger. They saw Numitor every day. He told more stories of earlier days in the kingdom. In his words, they came to know the mother who had left them so long ago.

Word spread that the grandsons of Numitor lived. There was talk of returning the throne to Numitor. It reached the ears of Antony. He was now old and feeble. He did not want to fight. He slipped away one night. He never was heard from again. Numitor retook the throne. The people were overjoyed. They held a huge celebration.

Numitor began his second rule. The twins wanted to find their own ways in the world. They did not want to live in the city of their forefathers. They started anew. "We'll build our own city," they said. "It will mark the spot where we were saved from death."

The spot where the wolf had found the twins was where the Tiber River flowed past a hill. The hill was one of seven. It was Palatine Hill. The twins went there. They looked out from the top of the hill. They saw the land below it. "It's beautiful," said Remus.

"It is," said Romulus. "We'll make our home on this hill."

They built a house. It was big. It was beautiful. After it was finished, Romulus wanted to build another. They did. When they finished, Romulus wanted to build another house. Remus did not. He was restless. He wanted to spend time in the nearby woods. He wanted to run and play with wolves.

Romulus built the next house without Remus. He did not stop. He built more and more houses. Remus helped at times, but mostly, he was with the wolves. He liked them. He was happy with them.

The houses grew into a city. The brothers ruled together at first. Then, the land had to be divided. They went to Numitor. He told them what to do.

"Watch for a sign," he said. "The gods will send it. The sign will tell us who will have the larger share of land. He will rule the city in the end. Go now. Wait for the gods."

The twins returned to their city. They waited. They did not know what the sign would be. On the second day, a flock of birds flew over the city. Six flew over Remus's home. Twelve flew over Romulus's. It was the sign.

Romulus turned to his twin. "The gods have spoken. I will rule the larger part of the city for now. I will rule all the city in time."

Remus was unhappy. He said, "The gods have looked unkindly on me. It will be as you wish. But, I will not share the city with you. You can rule it all now!" He left without looking back.

Romulus was sad. He did not like the way things had happened. He wanted to share the city with his twin. It was not to be. Remus went to live with the wolves.

Romulus ruled alone. It was a beautiful city. People came from far away to live there. They came for a better life. Some had been slaves. They lived in freedom there. Some had lived in poor homes. Romulus gave them new ones. He was kind. He and his people were happy. They loved him. He loved them.

The city was called Rome. It was named after the kind ruler whom the people loved. He was Romulus, the twin brother of Remus. They were the founders of Rome.

Don't Let Your Babies Grow Up to Be Roman Soldiers

"I'm so glad you're home," Titus said to his father.

"I'm very glad to be home," said his father. "It was a long, hard trip."

"Where did you go, Father?" Titus asked. He helped his father put away his army gear. Titus's father was a fighter. He fought with the cavalry. It was a group in the Roman army. He rode a horse. He carried a long spear. It had a sharp point at the end. It was called a javelin.

"We went all the way to northern England. We helped men who are building Hadrian's Wall," said his father. "They were fighters, too."

"Why did you have to go if there were other soldiers there, Father?"

"We were the auxiliary troops, Titus. We did not help build the wall. We protected the soldiers who worked on the wall."

"Is it a long way to England?" the boy asked.

"Yes," said his father, "it took many months to make the trip. We had to cross mountains. We had to fight many of the emperor's foes." Enemis

"What's this, Father?" asked Titus. He held up his father's kit.

"That holds all the things a soldier needs. They keep me safe. They help me do my job. Bring it here. I'll show you how each thing is used," the man said.

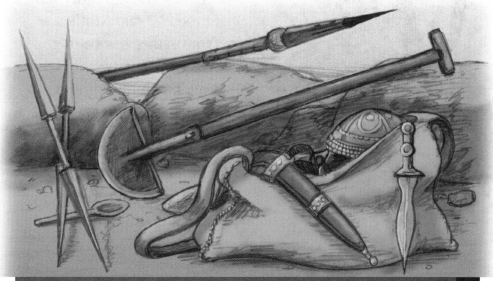

Titus handed the kit to him. He pulled out a wooden stake. It had a pointed end. "This is a palisade stake, Titus. We use it to build fences. We build around the place where we spend the night. It keeps out wild animals. It keeps people from stealing from us."

He took out a turf cutter next. "This is a digging tool. Sometimes, we dig trenches."

Then, he took out his mess tin. "This," he said, "is most important to many of us."

"What is it?" asked Titus.

"It's a mess tin. I keep my food in here," laughed his father.

"I want to see weapons, Father," said Titus.

"I will show you, Titus, but they are very dangerous. You must never touch them unless I am with you." The man held up a dagger. "This small knife has a very sharp blade. You must never touch it."

"I want to fight for Rome when I grow up," said Titus. The family sat down to dinner.

"There are many kinds of soldiers, Titus," said his father. "It's not easy to be in the Roman army."

"That's enough army talk for today," said Mother. "Your father has been gone a long time, Titus. He has come far to return home to us. You must not spend all his time talking about tools, weapons, and armor."

"I do not mind, Dear," said the man. "I've missed my son. I've missed his many questions."

The next day the father and son went for a ride on the father's horse. The horse was called Jupiter. "Why did you name him Jupiter, Father?" asked Titus.

"Jupiter is a god. He rules the thunder and lightning. I wanted to give you that name when you were born. You were loud as thunder. You were bright as lightning. But, your mother did not like the name. So, I named my horse Jupiter instead."

"I'll name my horse Jupiter when I join the army," said Titus.

"Remember what I said, Titus. There are many jobs in the Roman army," his father said. "You may not be in the cavalry."

"I won't go if I can't have a horse. I want a horse like Jupiter," declared the boy.

"Soldiers don't always have choices, Titus," said his father. "They must serve a long time. It can be 25 years. Many at Hadrian's Wall were builders at the milecastles. Some were guards."

"What are milecastles?" Titus asked.

"They are guard posts. They are built along the wall," said Father. "The guards stand watch day and night at the milecastles."

"Is that what they do all day?" asked Titus.

"Yes," said Father, "the builders have to cut and carry large rocks. The guards have to stand watch all day."

"That sounds boring to me," said Titus.

"Yes, and it's very hard work, too," the man replied.

"Are there other kinds of soldiers?" asked Titus.

"Yes, some men are foot soldiers. They walk for miles to battle. They build camps when they stop. They dig ditches and pile up the earth. They use palisade stakes to make fences. Then, they pitch their tents for the night. Their spears and shields are always ready for battle," said his father.

"Why do they carry shields?" asked Titus.

"To keep them safe, Titus. They sometimes group together. They hold their shields like a big tortoise shell."

"I bet that looks funny," laughed Titus.

Father shook his head. He said, "It may look funny, Titus. But, going into battle is not funny. Many men are forced to be in the army. They dream of leaving. They want to go home."

"I want to ride Jupiter again. How long will you be home this time?" the boy asked.

"I will be home forever, my son. My time is up in the army. I do not have to leave again."

The child hugged his father. "Never again? You never have to leave again?"

"That's right," smiled Father.

"I still want to be in the army when I grow up," Titus said. They rode back to the house.

"Don't tell your mother," smiled the man. "She wants both of her men home forever. Look, there she is waiting for us now."

Titus jumped down from the horse. He ran to his mother. "Mother! Mother! Father never has to leave us again," he yelled.

"I know," grinned his mother. "My men will be home with me forever."

LIFE IN ANCIENT ROME

People in ancient Rome lived busy lives. In some ways, they lived like people who live today. In some ways, their lives were different.

All in the Family

All family members lived together in the early days of Rome. Great-grandparents, grandparents, parents, and children lived in the same house. The head of the family was the father of the children.

Each family had rules. Each had customs. The main rule was that children must obey their father. He could put them out of the house if they did not. But, he had to answer for any wrong they did.

Mothers had important jobs. They had to see that the work was done around the house. They took care of the children. They trained servants. Girls learned to be good wives from their mothers.

Older family members were loved and cared for. They spent time playing with the children when they were too old to work. They went to the baths. They went to the theater.

Rich Roman families paid tutors. Tutors came to their homes to teach the boys to read. They taught them to write, too. Boys' schools were set up in some places. Girls went to school when they were older. Poor children rarely learned to read and write.

Home Sweet Home

Life in Rome was very different for the rich and the poor. The poor lived in apartments. They were called flats. The flats were above stores or shops on the streets. Large families sometimes crowded into a few rooms. Many flats had no kitchens. They had no water. The people ate food cooked in stalls on the street. They carried water from fountains.

The rich lived well. Many lived in town homes. Most were made of bricks. They had red tile roofs. They had courtyards with rooms around them. Paintings hung on the walls. Pictures called mosaics were on the floors. Many houses had running water and heat.

The rich often moved to the country in the summer. They had large homes called villas. They went to the country to get away from the heat and the crowds.

Eat, Drink, and Be Merry

The people ate simple foods. Mothers cooked meals. Female slaves did, too. Sometimes families sat on stools around tables in the courtyard to eat.

They did not have knives. They did not have forks. They had spoons. Food was cut into small bits before it was served. People ate with their fingers or spoons.

Most people ate three meals a day. The first was bread and fruit. Lunch was a light snack. It was most likely bread, vegetables, and meat. Dinner was the main meal. It was eaten in late afternoon. Poor people ate foods like hot pies from the street stalls. The pies were like pizzas. They had toppings like onions, fish, and olives. They did not have tomatoes. Tomatoes were not found in Rome until many years later.

Rich Romans had feasts. Guests were served fancy foods. They ate salads, eggs, and fish. Servants brought foods, such as baked flamingo. They served roasted pigs sometimes. The pigs were stuffed with dormice.

The guests did not sit on chairs. They lay on couches around the table. Some drank water. Others drank wine and water. Slaves carried snow from the tops of mountains to cool drinks on hot days.

Hi Ho, Hi Ho: Off to Work We Go

Three classes of people lived in early Rome. The rich men made the laws. They were called the ruling class. They were lawyers, army officers, and bankers. Some were merchants. They owned ships and shops. The ruling class ruled over the other people. They owned country villas. They had chariots and slaves.

The people who did most of the work were the working class. Stonemasons built homes and other buildings. Other people made things of wood and metal. Soldiers built roads and aqueducts. Other people made pottery and laid tiles.

These workers built Rome. They made the cities and roads. They fed the people with their crops. They built aqueducts to carry water to homes and baths. They worked on ships that sailed far away to get goods.

Many Romans worked for little or no pay. They were men, women, and children who had been sold as slaves. Some worked in homes and were treated like family. Others were treated badly. Slaves did the hardest and dirtiest jobs. They had no freedom and few rights.

Let Me Entertain You

Romans liked to have fun. They played games at home. They went to plays. They watched sports in big arenas.

Children had toys. Some were seesaws, swings, and kites. Others were hoops and toy houses. They played a game called knucklebones. It was like dice. Another game was draughts. It was like checkers.

Older Romans enjoyed races. They went to a place called the Circus Maximus. It was a big racetrack. Thousands of people went there. Chariots raced. Chariots were small two-wheeled carts. Fast horses pulled them. The drivers were mostly slaves. Their owners made them drive. The people in the stands cheered for their favorites. Drivers and horses sometimes were hurt. The races were dangerous, but popular.

Another sport was the gladiator fights. They were held at the Colosseum. It was a huge theater. Slaves or prisoners had to fight each other. Some fought wild animals. Lions and bears were shipped in to fight. Slave gladiators might be freed if they won matches.

The Romans enjoyed plays. They stood because there were no seats in the early days. Stone seats like steps were built later. Some plays were funny. They had happy endings. Some plays were sad.

Romans played and watched sports. They held contests at the Forum. There were foot races. Some people tried to be the best at javelin throwing. Others used bows and arrows. Only men and boys played. Women did not.

Men and boys went to the baths after the games. Women went to the baths, too. The baths had hot and cold pools. They had towels and steam rooms. The bathhouse was not just a place to bathe. People went there to exercise and play games. They met their friends to relax after work. Some baths had reading rooms, shops, and cafes.

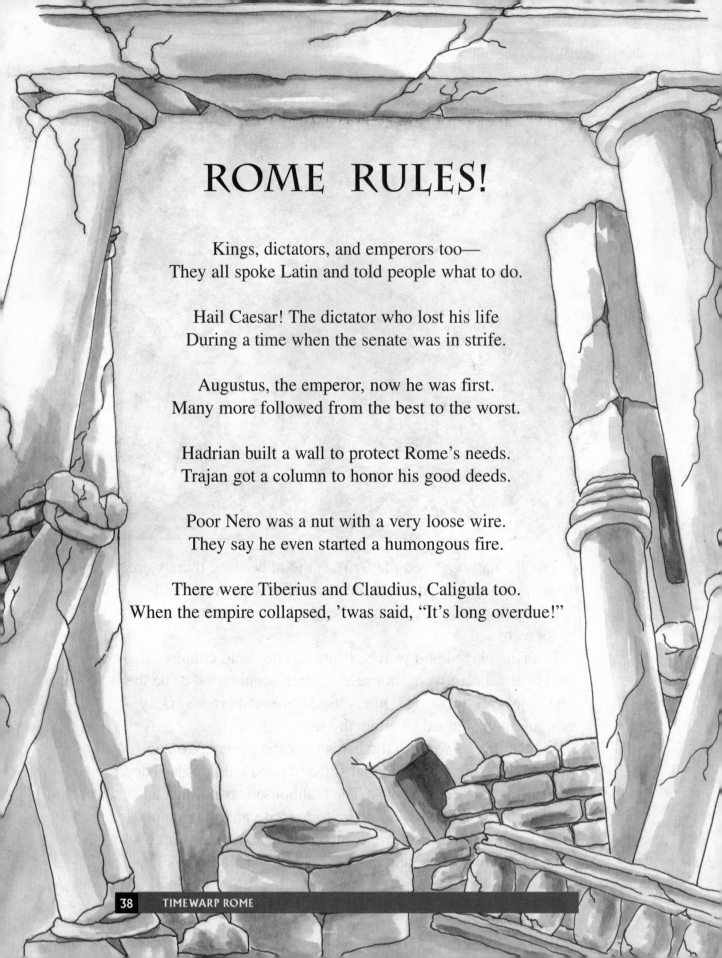

ROME RULES!

Kings, dictators, and emperors too—
They all spoke Latin and told people what to do.

Hail Caesar! The dictator who lost his life
During a time when the senate was in strife.

Augustus, the emperor, now he was first.
Many more followed from the best to the worst.

Hadrian built a wall to protect Rome's needs.
Trajan got a column to honor his good deeds.

Poor Nero was a nut with a very loose wire.
They say he even started a humongous fire.

There were Tiberius and Claudius, Caligula too.
When the empire collapsed, 'twas said, "It's long overdue!"

ROMAN
GODS AND GODDESSES

The Romans believed in gods and goddesses. They thought the gods and goddesses had magic powers. The gods and goddesses were strong. They ruled over the people's lives. The people wanted to keep them happy.

THE SHINING FATHER

Jupiter called out, "I am the greatest god. I am the most powerful. You will obey me, or I will punish you!" Jupiter would not let the people of Rome forget his power. He reminded them day and night. He was the god of the sky. He was the god of thunder and lightning. No other gods or goddesses were as strong.

Romans were awed by his control of the weather. Once Jupiter was angry with the people of Rome. They were being unkind to one another. He did not like it. He sent a thunderstorm to punish them. Rain fell for days. There were great floods. A big bolt of lightning came down. It went from the sky to the ground as far as the eye could see. It hit a huge olive tree. It burned for days. Then, it was charred. It had no leaves. A few twisted branches were left. The tree was left standing. People who walked by remembered the power of Jupiter. They remembered to be kind to one another.

Pictures show Jupiter as a great bearded man. He sits on a throne. He holds a lightning bolt in one hand. He has a scepter in the other. It is a long stick. An eagle often soars above him.

PROTECTOR OF THE LEGIONS

Mars was important to Roman soldiers. They honored him. He was the god of war. He was the god of battle. Mars was believed to care for the fighters. They called themselves sons of Mars.

Some said Mars was the son of Jupiter. They said he was the father of Romulus and Remus. They called him the grandfather of Rome.

Sounds of war were said to please Mars. He liked to hear the zing of spears. He liked to hear battle cries. He used his power to start wars. He made the fighters want to go into battle. People thought battles were won or lost because of him.

Parades were held for him. One was a parade of jumpers. They sang and jumped from the beginning to the end of the parade.

The month of March was on the Roman calendar. It was named for Mars. The fourth planet from the sun was named after the god, too.

Mars is shown as a fighter. He wears armor. He has a spear in one hand.

RULER OF THE SEA

Romans believed that Jupiter had a brother. His name was Neptune. Neptune was powerful, too. He ruled the oceans. It was said that he gave the first horse to man.

Jupiter lived in the sky. Neptune lived in the sea. His home was a palace.

People thought Neptune commanded the wind. They thought he could make storms at sea. If sailors did not honor him, they believed waves would destroy their ships. They feared sea monsters might rise up to attack. They thought Neptune calmed terrible storms. He saved the lives of many seamen. Romans spoke to Neptune. They said, "Oh, great Neptune, you are truly the ruler of the deep."

In pictures, Neptune may be standing in a huge seashell cart. A team of horses pulls it. He holds a trident in one hand. It is a spear with three prongs.

HUNTRESS AND PROTECTOR

Women revered Diana. She was the goddess of the moon. She was said to rule the mountains of Rome. She ruled the countryside. She protected the woods.

People believed Diana ruled the wild animals. She was a great huntress. A good hunt meant she was near. Hunters took time to thank her.

It was said she saved hunters from danger in the woods. One story told of a young woman who worshiped Diana. She liked the forest. She liked hunting. One day, the woman was in danger. She ran, but was chased. She prayed to Diana. Diana spoke, "You are in danger no more." The woman turned into a spring of water. She was saved from harm.

Pictures show Diana with a golden bow. She has silver arrows. It is said the deer was her favorite animal. It often is shown with her.

DOORKEEPER OF THE OLD AND NEW

Janus was the keeper of doors and gates. He stood for the beginning and end of each year. The month of January was named for him.

It was said he came from the Underworld as a baby. He did not look like other gods. He hid. He knew his looks would scare people.

One story told of a shepherd boy who saw Janus. He did not run. He was not afraid. He said, "You do not frighten me. I will be your friend. You will not be alone." People heard about the friendship. They began to visit Janus. They took him food and gifts.

Jupiter told Janus he could become a god. He gave him power over doors and gates. He gave him power over the beginning and end of the year.

Janus's temple let people know if war was ahead. Open temple doors meant war. Closed doors were for peace.

Festivals were held for Janus at the end of each year. Coins were exchanged. They showed the head of Janus.

Pictures show Janus as a man with two faces. One face looks to the future. The other looks to the past.

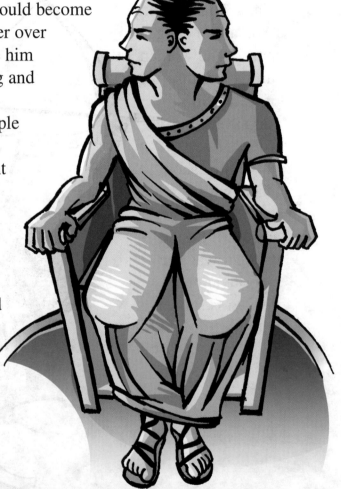

THE DOCTOR'S DOCTOR

Romans said Minerva was Jupiter's daughter. She ruled over wisdom and medicine. She was said to have invented numbers and musical instruments. Doctors and healers worshiped her. They built her temple on a hill outside Rome.

Minerva was said to help doctors. She helped sick people, too. There is a tale of a rich man's daughter who was sick for a year. She could not eat. She could not lift her head. A healer tried everything to heal her. The healer called on Minerva. He said, "Please help this child. I can do no more."

The child was healed. The healer and the father thanked Minerva. They left gifts at her temple. The child was said to improve each time a gift was left there. She became healthy.

The people held festivals for Minerva. Doctors and healers were there. People who had been made well were there, too.

Minerva looks like a warrior. She carries a spear. She holds a shield.

GROWER OF SEEDS

The Romans had a god of farming. He was Saturn. He ruled over the sowing of seeds. He protected crops.

Romans thought Saturn was Jupiter's father. They said that one day Jupiter grew angry with him. Jupiter said, "You have angered the most powerful one. Go away. Never return." Jupiter chased Saturn away. Janus took him in. Saturn learned to make seeds grow. Farmers worshiped him. They thanked him for good harvests.

The Golden Age was a good time in Rome. There was peace. There was happiness. It was because crops grew well.

Each year a festival was held for Saturn. It lasted for seven days. It was in December. Shops closed. Slaves changed places with masters. The masters served the slaves. People gave gifts. They gave money to loved ones.

Saturday is named for Saturn. One of the planets is named for him. It is next to Jupiter.

Saturn carries a tool in many pictures. It is a scythe. It is used for harvesting.

Why the Seasons Change:
A Myth of Ancient Rome

Once there was a young girl. Her name was Proserpina. She lived when the gods still walked upon the earth. Her father was Jupiter. He was king of the gods. Her mother was Ceres. She was the goddess of fruits and vegetables.

The girl's friends called her Pina. She liked to run and play with the young wood maidens. The maidens were called nymphs. They roamed the woods and meadows. They picked flowers. They made belts and necklaces with the flowers. The girls laughed as they played together.

One day, Pina and her friends were playing in the meadow. A big black cloud appeared. It hung over them.

"We must hurry home, Pina," cried a nymph. "It's getting dark. I am afraid."

"Run, everyone," shouted Pina. The girls left their flowers on the grass. They ran.

Suddenly, the cloud lifted. The girls could not believe their eyes. "Look," shouted Pina. They turned. They saw a beautiful chariot. Two black horses pulled it. It flew across the sky like a comet.

"Oh, Pina," said one nymph, "it is Dis. We must get away quickly."

"Who is he?" asked Pina. "I do not know him."

"Dis is the king of the Underworld," said the nymph. "He is evil. He is wicked."

The chariot swooped down from the sky. Dis saw Pina. He could not believe his eyes. He knew who she was. She was thought to be the most beautiful girl in the world.

Dis thought, "I will make her my wife."

"Proserpina, come away with me," he called. "Come away with me. I will make you happy for the rest of your days."

"No," cried Pina, "I will never go with you. You are evil."

She ran as fast as she could. Dis was much faster and stronger. He came down from the sky in his chariot. He reached for Proserpina. They went into the black cloud. Then, they went to the Underworld.

Pina cried. She begged Dis to take her home. He put her in a dark, gloomy room. He left her. Day after day, servants brought food for her. She did not eat. She grew weaker and weaker.

Ceres was heartsick for her daughter. She spent days walking in the meadows. She searched everywhere. She cried out in her sleep, "Oh my darling daughter, where can you be?"

One day, she found a small belt. It was made with the tears of the nymphs. It floated in a small lake in the meadow. It made Ceres sadder. She was so sad that she forgot to take care of the fruits and vegetables of the world. The people of Earth began to starve.

"You must not be sad, Ceres," said Jupiter. "You have work to do. The people are hungry."

"I will tend the crops if you bring my child home," Ceres said to Jupiter.

"I have searched," said Jupiter. "I have searched the world over. I cannot find her."

At that, one of Jupiter's soldiers came into the room. "We know what has become of her," the man said. "Dis took Proserpina from the meadow."

"I should have known," said Jupiter. "He has taken her to the Underworld. If she eats food there, she can never come back to us," he said.

Meanwhile, Dis visited Pina every day. He pleaded with her to eat. "You must eat," he said. "You will die if you do not." Pina shook her head sadly. She refused any food offered to her. This upset Dis.

One day, Dis was so upset that he lied. He told Pina he would let her go if she ate something. "Eat these pomegranate seeds. I promise I will let you go," he said. She ate the seeds.

The next day, Dis rode his horses across the sky. Jupiter threw a bolt of lightning at him. "You must return my daughter, Dis," he demanded.

Dis flashed an evil smile. "I cannot," Dis said. "She has eaten six pomegranate seeds." He laughed.

Jupiter knew Dis had tricked Pina. There was nothing he could do. Then, he had an idea. "You may keep her six months each year," said Jupiter. "I will have her for the other six."

Dis knew he had to obey. Jupiter would never leave him alone. "Yes," said Dis, "I agree."

Pina was returned to Ceres. Earth began to look brighter. Trees began to sprout leaves. Fruits and vegetables grew. The world was warm and friendly. But, this did not last forever. Jupiter and Dis had made a deal.

Pina had to return to the Underworld. When she did, Earth grew dark and cold again. It was said that this was how the seasons began. Pina was home with her mother in summer and spring. She returned to Dis in the fall and winter.

Helena:
Roman Empress

Helena was a young girl. She lived far from the city of Rome. Her family was very poor. Helena did not marry when she was older. She had to work. She worked in a place that served beer and food. It was like a tavern. It was not a good place for a young girl to work. But Helena had to work. Her family needed the money for food. Then, the Romans came.

The Romans were now the rulers. They built homes and forts. They made laws. They helped the people, too. Still, some people were angry. They were angry that the Romans had taken over their land. They wanted to rule themselves. Others were glad. The Romans brought with them new types of foods and goods. They taught people how to read and write. The Romans built roads from one small town to the next. The Roman army protected the towns.

Helena got to know a few of the Romans who came to eat where she worked. She liked the Romans. They made life easier for the people.

One day she met a young Roman officer. His name was Constantius. They liked each other very much. He got to know her and her family. She got to know him and his friends. Soon they fell in love. However, he was a famous Roman officer. She was a poor, tavern girl. That didn't stop their love. Soon, they had their own home.

Constantius and Helena lived in their small home for twelve years. They were very happy. Helena no longer had to work in the tavern. Constantius helped Helena's family. Constantius and Helena had a baby. They called him Constantine. He was their only child. Constantius was sad. He knew that soon he would have to leave. He would have to go back to Rome. He knew that Helena could not go with him. The citizens of Rome would not accept her as his wife. He did not want his life with Helena to end.

One day it happened. Constantius was told to return to Rome. He was now the Caesar of the Western Roman Empire. He was told to give up his life with Helena. He had to marry someone else. She was the daughter of the other Caesar. Constantine was sent to live with another ruler. He would go to school. He would learn how to be a ruler.

Years passed. Constantius was a good ruler. Constantine grew to be a smart young man. He was a good general in the army. Constantius asked if Constantine could come home. The other Caesar said yes. For the first time in more than thirteen years, Constantine saw his father. It had been a long time. Constantine and his father worked together to help the people. They went to battle together to fight the enemy. Then, Constantius died.

When Constantius died, Constantine took his place. Constantine was now Caesar. Helena now had honor and respect. The people knew she was Constantine's mother. She joined his court. He named her "Most Honored and Noble Lady." Helena's picture was put on coins. Helena helped Constantine. She helped him do things better. She worked hard to help people. The people loved her. Helena became the empress. She was no longer the young girl in the tavern. She was now the most powerful woman in the land.

Julius Caesar
and the Pirates

It was hot yesterday. It is hot today. On the boat, Julius sits in the cool breeze. He fans himself with a large piece of paper. He does not like it when it is hot. He looks around and smiles. He is on his way to the island of Rhodes! Julius wants to go to school there. It is a good school for young men. He wants to learn how to give

speeches. Julius knows it is important to learn how to give speeches. He hopes to be a good leader in his country. Maybe someday he will be the leader of the Roman Empire. Right now he just wants to learn. He is finally old enough.

The sleek boat moves quickly over the deep, blue water. The big sails fill with the warm wind. White birds fly around the boat. Julius is excited. He has never gone so far before. He wants the boat to go faster. Then he sees boats in the distance. The boats do not look like the one he is on. They do not have the same sails. He does not know who the men on the boats are. The men on Julius's boat become upset. They say the boats are pirate ships. Julius does not want to be taken by pirates. The boats come closer. They are pirate ships! The pirates throw heavy ropes with hooks onto Julius's ship. The men on Julius's boat fight back. The pirates are bigger. There are more of them. They win the fight. They take Julius's ship. They take the money on the ship. They take the food and water. They also take Julius!

The pirates take Julius onto their ship. They will not let him go. They want money. He does not have any. They say they will ask his family for money. When they get it, they will let Julius go.

Julius is angry, but he is smart. He does not fight with the pirates. He listens to them. He finds out how much money they want. It isn't very much. Julius tells them to ask for more. Then, people will think he is a very important man. The pirates cannot believe it. They think about it. They do as he says.

Julius is on the pirate ship for almost 40 days. It is very hot. It is crowded. He sleeps on the deck. It is hard wood. There are no beds. There is little food or water.

The pirates are unhappy. They fight. They sail the waters waiting to hear about the money. Sometimes they have to hide from other ships. They hide in bays and inlets. The other ships are trying to capture the pirates. Julius hopes they will get caught, but the pirates always escape. They are very good at escaping.

Julius learns the names of the pirates. He wants to remember who they are. He jokes with them. Julius tells them that someday he will be important. He will have money. Then he will hire someone to come after them. The pirates laugh. They do not believe Julius. He is only one small man.

They are big men. There are many of them. No one can catch them in their fast boat! The pirates think they are safe.

At last the pirates get the money for Julius. His family pays a lot for his freedom. The pirates are happy. They let Julius go. He is free to go home or to school.

Julius changes his mind. He does not go to school. He hires men to help him catch the pirates. Now Julius is the one chasing the pirates. The pirates' ship is fast. Julius's ship is faster. They try to hide. Julius knows where they hide.

Julius catches the pirates. He takes back the money. He takes the pirates to Rome. They must pay for their crimes. Julius is happy to be free. He can now do what he wants to do. He can even go to school!

The Day the Mountain Roared

Long ago, there was a town called Pompeii. It was in Italy. It stood at the foot of a great mountain. The mountain was called Vesuvius.

The people of the town liked living near the mountain. The land around it was rich. It let them grow grapes and many other crops. Their animals ate well from the land. They lived in strong houses that kept out wind and rain. They were at peace with their neighbors.

One day, the sun rose high over Pompeii. The people began to stir. The marketplace opened. People began to trade goods. Some bought things. Others sold them. Carts bumped along the streets. The people shouted to one another.

The sounds of the marketplace awoke families. They lived in the houses near it. Mothers and fathers began to start the day. Some mothers prayed. Then, they started their house duties. Some fathers headed out to fish. Others went to the fields to tend crops. Children ate breakfast. Afterward, they went out to play in the sun.

Outside, the children smelled bread baking. They stopped to watch potters and weavers at work. They skipped along behind slaves who carried water.

At the bathhouse, men played games. Some sat in the steam room. Others soaked in hot pools of water. They laughed and talked together.

The day had begun like most others in Pompeii. It would not end the same. It would be very different. Pompeii would be changed forever. The people had no idea what was ahead.

Later in the morning, a rumbling was heard. Old Cradus heard it. He did not like the sound. He stepped outside his shop. He looked out at the mountain. Smoke rose from its top.

Cradus had lived a long time. He knew that what he saw was bad. The village was in danger. He ran at once to the town meeting place.

Lawmakers were busy. They were making new laws. They had not heard the noise. Cradus ran among them. "The mountain rumbles," he warned. "It is angry. It will soon roar. It will spew out hot mud. It will choke us with ash. We will be covered. We will die if we do not leave the town at once."

The lawmakers were unmoved. Cradus had lived a long time. They thought him to be foolish in his old age. "He speaks of the mountain as if it were a great lion," they laughed. One man began to prance around and roar like a lion. The others laughed.

Another man said, "No, it is not the roar of a lion, but that of a dragon." He ran around the room. He waved his arms like wings. "Hear my dragon's roar," he said. He laughed until he began to choke. The others joined his laughter.

Cradus left the meeting place. He ran through the streets. He shouted to all who would hear. "Leave now, while you still can. You soon will hear the mountain roar. Go to the sea. It will save you."

Many people saw Cradus. They knew him. He was old. They smiled kindly at him and went on their way.

The sun crept higher in the sky. The rumble became louder. Then, there was a great boom from the mountain. The smoke thickened. The people turned to look.

Suddenly, hot mud shot into the sky. It began to flow down the side of the mountain. It flowed very fast. The people screamed. They began to run. They left everything behind them.

The cloud of smoke blocked the sun. The town was dark. The mountain began to spray more mud on the town. Some people ran to their homes to hide. Some went to the temples. They prayed that the gods would save them. A few remembered what Cradus had said. They found him at the seashore. They joined him as he headed out to sea. They looked back at the town.

The hot mud flowed over the town. It covered buildings. It covered people. Ashes rained down on them. The people could not escape. At last, the mountain sent out a blast of hot gas. It was like poison. It covered the town like a cloud. Everyone was gone.

For two more days, ashes piled on top of Pompeii. Then, the mountain fell silent. The cloud of gas and smoke went away. Pompeii was silent, too. Those who had not gone to the sea were dead.

Cradus and the others at sea went back to the shore. They wanted to see what was left of their town. There was almost nothing. Only the tops of buildings were seen. Pompeii was buried. Their town was gone. It was lost the day the mountain roared.

The Herculaneum Rap

Did you know there was another town like Pompeii
That suffered just as much on that frightful day?

There was food and music for the crowds at the fair.
Little did they know that there was danger in the air!

Without a warning came a thunderous sound.
Poison ash and gases came tumbling to the ground.

People ran to the ocean, but they could not get away.
They were trapped, and they died on that horrible day.

Besides Pompeii, there's Herculaneum we know,
Where it rained fire so many years ago.

All Roads Lead to Rome

Romans were inventors. They were builders. They had ideas for making buildings bigger. They had ways of making them safer.

They invented the arch. It made buildings stronger. It gave beauty. They invented aqueducts. They carried water into homes and fountains. Romans made straight roads. The roads were paved with stone.

Romans liked big things. They liked things to work well. The engineers were well trained. They had soldiers and slaves to help them. They did not worry how long it took to build something. They did not worry about costs. They did the best job they could.

Roman Roads

Roads made the empire strong. They let armies move quickly from spot to spot. Traders and farmers brought goods in and out of cities. The roads made it quick and easy.

Romans built roads. They built them wherever they went. All roads led to and from the city of Rome. It was the center of Roman life.

The early roads were mud tracks. They led over or around hills. Engineers looked for straight flat spots. They were the best spots to build roads. Builders put milestones at the roadsides. Milestones let people know far they had gone. A Roman mile was 1,000 paces. A pace is a man's step.

Building roads was a process. First, a short, flat route was found. The land was cleared of trees. Rocks were removed. The workers dug a trench. It was 3 feet deep. They filled it with stones of all sizes. The top layer had a mound or lump in the middle. The mound let rain run into ditches. The roads were well made. Many exist to this day.

Arches and Aqueducts

Romans made a kind of concrete. It was very strong. They mixed lime, water, and volcano ash. The mixture dried hard as stone. It stayed strong. It even worked underwater.

Romans invented the arch. It helped them build bigger buildings. No one had been able to do this before them.

Another great invention was the aqueduct. Aqueducts looked like bridges. They did not have roads on top. There were channels to carry water. Romans used them to get water from mountain streams. They brought water to the cities. The people had baths. They had toilets. They had fountains. Many pictures showed aqueducts above ground. Most of them were really built underground.

Much was left when the empire ended. Buildings remained. Mosaics were found. Writings could be read. Paintings could be studied. Many roads still could be traveled. Weapons survived after the soldiers were gone. What remained told much about the Romans and how they lived.

Can You Dig It?

"We're going to Italy. We're going to Italy!" yelled Max and Lara.

"I've never seen them act like that," said Grandpa.

"I've been telling them about the town you grew up in, Dad," said Marco. He was Max and Lara's father. "The museum is sending me there to a dig. That means Patty and the children can go, too. We can see where you grew up, and I can get some work done."

"When are we going, Dad?" asked Max.

"School will be out next week," Dad said. "We'll leave the week after that."

"Is Mom going, too?" asked Lara.

"Yes," said Dad, "she's getting off work to go with us."

"Yea!" shouted Max and Lara. They danced around the room.

Lara and Max's dad was an archaeologist. He worked all over the world. He looked for clues about how people lived long ago.

"Will you have to work while we're there, Dad?" asked Lara.

"Yes," he said, "you will get to see a real dig."

"What's that mean, Dad?" asked Max. "What's a dig?"

"A dig is a place where workers dig up things from the past," said Dad. "But first, we have to make a list of what we need to take on our trip."

The next day, Dad took Max and Lara to a shop. They each got a toolbox and a hard hat. They got notebooks, too.

"What will we put in our toolboxes, Daddy?" asked Lara.

"When we get to the dig, I'll give you some tools. You'll use them to work," he answered.

The trip to Italy was long. It made them tired. Finally, they made it to a hotel. It was in a place called Pompeii.

"Is this Grandpa's town?" asked Lara.

"No," said Dad, "but it is not far from here."

At last, the big day came. They took a taxi. They went to a small village. It was not far from Pompeii. They met Dad's Uncle Tony. They met his wife, Maria, too. "That is the school that your Grandpa went to," said Uncle Tony.

"I wish Grandpa had come with us," said Lara. "He could have taken us everywhere."

"I wanted him to come, Lara," said Mom, "but he has not been well. We'll take a lot of pictures. That will make him happy."

The family visited Grandpa's old home. They went to his school. They went to a shop where he worked as a boy. Then, they took a taxi back to Pompeii. After dinner, they talked about the next day. They talked about what they would do. "We'll visit the Roman ruins and the dig site where my crew is working," said Dad. "It will be a fun day. You'll see."

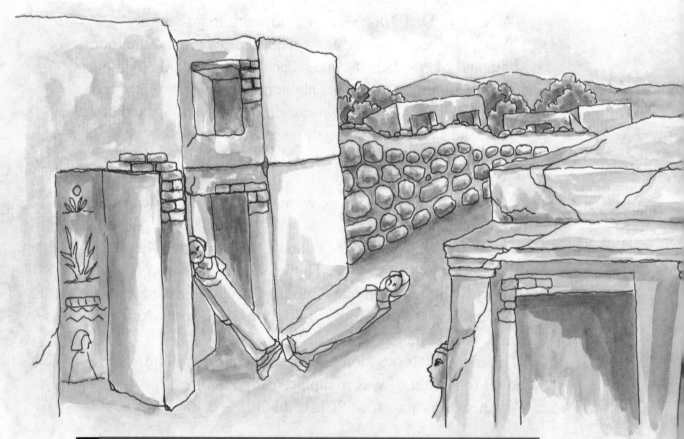

"Look, kids," said Mom. She pointed out the taxi window. "That's a volcano. It erupted long ago. That means it blew up. It was in the glory days of Rome. It covered Pompeii with ash. The whole town was covered for hundreds of years."

"Did Grandpa get covered, too?" asked Lara.

"No," laughed Mom, "Grandpa is not that old."

"How did they find the town, Mom?" asked Max.

"Farmers were working in the fields. They started digging," she said. "They found things that made them see that a town had been there. Now, men like your father dig up more things. That is how we find out about life in old Roman times."

Soon, they came to a busy spot. Many people were walking around it. "We'll see the remains of the town here," said Dad.

They got out of the taxi and started walking. They saw walls and doorways of homes. The homes were thousands of years old. They walked on roads built by Romans. They saw statues of men and women. "Look, Mom," said Lara. "They painted pictures on the walls. They are still here."

The family went into a museum. It had hundreds of objects that were found at the site. They saw vases and pots. They saw dishes and spoons. They saw coins and rings. There were necklaces and earrings. There were lamps and hammers. There were also spears and picks.

"Did your workers find any of these, Dad?" asked Max.

"Most of these things were found years ago, Max," said Dad. "Tomorrow we will go to the spot where my crew is digging. I'm sure they'll have many things to show us."

The family spent the rest of the day seeing the city of Pompeii. They saw many old ruins. The children were tired at the end of the day.

The next morning, Dad said, "Get your toolboxes. I have some things for you." He opened a big box. It had been sent to the hotel. He gave each of them a trowel. It was for digging. He gave them small rakes and boxes of little brushes. "You're ready to be junior archaeologists," he said. "Let's go dig."

They walked to the site. "This is Cathy. She's the crew boss," said Dad.

"Hi, kids. Come with me," Cathy said. "I've been waiting for you. Put on your hard hat, Lara. All site workers wear hard hats." Cathy led the way to what looked like the floor of a house. It had been buried under tons of ash. The crew had just started looking for objects in the area. "Digging is like fishing," she said. "Some days you pull up a treasure. Some days you don't get a thing."

Cathy showed them how to carefully dig with the trowels. She showed them how to brush away dust and dirt with the brushes. She told them to write in their notebooks. They would list anything that they found.

"This is hard work," said Max after he had dug for awhile.

"Max, I found something," yelled Lara. "Look, it's part of a cow's horn."

"How do you know it's not something else?" asked Max.

"It looks like a cow's horn to me," said Lara.

"Don't pick it up," said Cathy. "Brush away the dirt. List it in your notebook."

It wasn't long before Max yelled, too. "Look, Cathy, it's a bit of blue tile."

"That was part of a floor, Max," Cathy said. "We know the kitchen of this house had a picture on the floor. It was a mosaic."

The children worked all morning. They found bits of pottery and tile. Lara found another bit of cow's horn.

At lunch, they told Mom and Dad what they learned about digging. They shared their notebooks. They told about the things they had found.

"You know," said Dad, "the best thing about digging is when you find something. You know that no one else has seen or held it for many years. That is something."

"What was the most important thing you learned today?" asked Mom. The family was on the way back to the hotel.

"I learned how hard Dad's job is," said Max.

"I learned how Romans lived long ago," said Lara. "They had cows back then, too."

I Love You As Much

Once there was a beautiful villa near Rome. In it lived a rich man and his three daughters. The girls loved their father very much. He loved them. He liked to hear them tell him how much they loved him.

Each girl tried to outdo the others in telling of her love for him. They played a game. It was called "I Love You As Much." Each girl named something that told how much she loved him. Each tried to think of the best thing.

The first daughter said, "I love you as much as Earth loves Sky." One day, she said, "I love you as much as my beautiful hair."

The second one said, "I love you as much as arms love hands." One day, she said, "I love you as much as my beautiful toes."

The third daughter said, "I love you as much as mice love cheese." One day, she said, "I love you as much as my pale cheeks."

The man liked the game. One day, he said once again, "Come. Tell me how much you love me."

The oldest girl said, "Papa, I love you as much as I love my eyes."

"That's a lot," the man said.

It was the second girl's turn. She thought for a time. Then, she said, "I love you as much as I love my heart."

"That's a lot of love!" smiled the man.

Last, it was the third and youngest daughter's turn. She thought for a time. Then she said, "I love you as much as water and salt."

"Water and salt!" exclaimed the father. "Those are not things to love. This is *pessime*, terrible! Who loves water and salt?" He was angry. He called the servants. He had them take away the girl.

She was taken to Trajan's Market. She was sold as a slave. For years, she worked as a slave for a wealthy family. One day, she told the family her story. They felt sorry for her. They set her free. She stayed with them. They loved her as one of the family.

Years later, the girl was to marry a son of the family. They planned a big wedding banquet. They invited the rich families from nearby villas. The bride knew her father would come.

Over the years, her father had aged. He had become ill. He was sorry for what he had said to her. He was sorry for sending her away from the home. He missed her more each day.

It was the day of the wedding. The man did not want to go. He wanted to stay home. He knew he must go.

All the rich people were there. The girl sat by her father. He had not seen her for years. He did not know her. She saw to it that salt and water were passed to everyone except her father. She saw that he did not eat. "*Domine*, is the meat not good?" she asked.

Her father replied, "*Ita est*, yes, I will eat. I'm sure it's fine." He tasted the meat. He did not like it. It had no salt. There was no water to wash it down. The man was unhappy.

Later, the people told stories at the wedding. The man told the story of his little daughter. He told how he missed her. He spoke of wanting her home.

His daughter left the room. Soon, she returned. She was dressed as she had been when she was sent away.

She said, "I said I loved you as much as water and salt. You sent me away. You have seen what it's like to eat without water and salt. Now, do you know my love, Papa?"

The man cried. He asked her to forgive him. She did. She said, "I love you as much as a daughter can love."

Her father replied, "Dear, I love you as much as a father can love."

The celebration began once more. Father and daughter were happy to be together again. The bride and groom went to live in a villa. It was near her father and sisters. They lived happily to the end of their days.

The Tatiana Doll

Once there was a man who had lost his wife. He lived with his daughter. Her name was Tatiana. He sent her to school. "Listen to the teacher," he said.

The teacher knew the girl's father. She wanted to marry him. Every day she said, "You need a mother. Your father needs a wife. Tell your father I will be a good mother. I will be a good wife."

Tatiana told him. He said, "*Non*, Tatiana. Another wife for me would not be good for you."

The teacher would not give up the idea. Tatiana kept telling her father. Finally, he agreed to marry the teacher.

Sadly, the man was right. It was not good for Tatiana. The teacher was mean. She treated Tatiana badly. Each day, she sent her out to find herbs. The place was on a cliff. It dropped off to the sea. If Tatiana fell, she would be lost forever.

Tatiana was very unhappy. She wept for her dead mother. She wept for her father. She wept for herself.

One day, a large bird saw her. It lit on the ground near her. "Why are you here? Why do you cry?" said the bird.

"I cry from fear. Each day I must come here to get herbs. I must go close to the edge of the cliff. I must find the herbs my stepmother wants. If I do not, she will be angry. I fear I will fall into the sea," Tatiana said.

The bird listened. It felt sorry for her. It said, "Climb on my back. I will take you away from here. I will save you from your stepmother. I will take you where you will be safe and happy."

The bird took Tatiana far away to a crystal villa. It was in the mountains. Fairies lived there. They saw Tatiana. They loved her at once. The bird left her there. The fairies cared for her.

Ten days later, the bird flew to the stepmother. It asked, "Where is your daughter?"

The stepmother smiled, "She is gone! I have not seen her for 10 days. Maybe the sea took her."

The bird was angry. It said, "Foolish woman, the sea did not take her. I took her. She is safe. She is happy." With that, the bird flew into the sky.

The stepmother was enraged. "I must be rid of the girl. She must never return. If her father learns what I did, all is lost."

The stepmother went to the city. There, she found a witch. She told the witch she wanted to be rid of Tatiana. She told what the bird had done. She asked the witch for help. The witch agreed to help. She made honey cakes. She cast a spell on them.

Meanwhile, the fairies learned that the stepmother had gone to see the witch. They knew she would try to harm the girl. They worried for they needed to go away for a few days. Tatiana could not go with them. They said to her, "Do not open the door of the crystal villa to anyone while we are gone. Your stepmother plans evil." Tatiana promised to do as she was told. The fairies left the villa.

The next day, there was a knock at the door. Tatiana recalled her promise. She did not open it. The knock grew louder. Tatiana could not ignore it. She looked through a small hole in the door.

She was surprised at what she saw. "It's a servant of my father," she thought. It was not.

The person at the door said, "Tatiana, your father misses you. He could not stop crying. A bird told him you were here. It said you were safe. Your father had me make you some honey cakes. He is overjoyed that you are alive."

Tatiana did not want to open the door. Surely, the servant spoke the truth. What harm could it do? She opened the door. The person wasted no time. She gave Tatiana the honey cakes. Tatiana tasted the cakes at once. She closed the door and fell to the floor.

The fairies returned in two days. They found Tatiana. They knew she had been tricked. It was the witch who had the honey cakes. The fairies wept. They begged the mother fairy to bring her back to life.

The mother fairy was not pleased. Tatiana had disobeyed. But, she agreed. She opened the girl's mouth. She took out the bite of cake. She waved her wand. Tatiana came back to life. She promised not to disobey again.

Soon, the fairies had to go away again. Tatiana promised not to open the door. She promised not to speak to anyone. "If you do not keep your word, I will not be able to save you," the mother fairy said.

Again, there was a knock at the door. It was the witch. She looked like the town dressmaker. "Open up, Tatiana," she said. "I have a new dress for you from the fairies."

Tatiana was confused. She had known the dressmaker all her life. She knew her voice. Surely, this was not a trick. The dressmaker said the fairies had sent her. Still, Tatiana called, "No, I cannot open the door. I have been tricked once. I can't be tricked again."

"This isn't a trick," said the witch. "You must put on your dress. You will be ready when the fairies return. You know me, child. I have always made your dresses."

Tatiana did not know what to do. Her heart pounded. Then, she opened the door. The dressmaker gave her a lovely dress. She helped Tatiana into it. Then, she left.

Tatiana tried to leave the dressing room. The dress became very heavy. Tatiana fell to the floor. She tumbled down the stairs in the heavy dress.

The fairies found her when they returned. Mother fairy was very angry. Tatiana had disobeyed again.

The mother fairy kept her word. She did not use her wand. She did not bring Tatiana back to life. Yet, she loved the girl as the other fairies did.

She pointed her wand. A crystal casket appeared around Tatiana. It was inlaid with diamonds. Other beautiful stones were on it, too. It also had flowers of silver and gold.

The mother fairy brought forth a horse to pull it. The horse was finer than any in the Roman Empire. She spoke to the other fairies. "Have the horse take the casket to the place I tell you. Leave the horse and casket there." To the horse, the mother fairy said, "When the fairies leave, run with the casket. Run as if your life depends on it. Do not stop until you hear, 'Please stop! I have given my best horse for you.'"

All was done as the mother fairy ordered. The horse was led to the center of the city. The fairies left it. The horse did as it was told. As it ran, it passed a young man on a horse. The man saw the horse. He quickly turned around and began chasing it. Finally, his horse could go no further. It had to stop. The young man jumped from his horse. He ran on foot. Soon, he could run no more. He called, "Please stop! I have given my best horse for you."

The beautiful horse stopped. The young man saw the crystal casket. He saw Tatiana. He took the horse and casket back to his villa.

When the young man's mother saw him, she did not know what to say. Her husband was dead. Her son ruled the villa.

"Mother," the young man said, "I have found a wife."

"Found a wife? This girl is beautiful, but she's dead," said his mother. "She is like a doll."

"It doesn't matter," he said. "She is my wife."

The young man put the casket in a room. He ate his meals there. He did not leave unless he had to do so.

One day, he had to go to war. He had to fight for the city. He asked his mother to take care of his wife.

He went to war. His mother paid no mind to the girl in the casket. "She is just a doll," she thought. Then, she learned that her son was returning. She was afraid. She called the servants. "Trouble comes," she said. "My son is returning. We have not cared for his doll. What will we do?"

They went to the room with the casket. The mother touched a diamond on it. It broke off and a small hole was where it had been. She tried to shove the diamond in the hole. It would not stay. She knew she must cover the hole before her son returned. She loved him. She did not want him to be sad or upset. She thought of what to do.

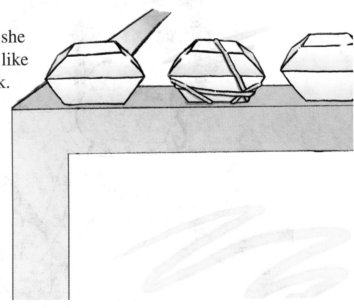

She took off her best gold necklace. She tied it over the diamond. She slipped her necklace into the hole. It would be heavy enough to hold the diamond in the hole.

When she did this, she heard a sound. It was like a key turning in a lock. She looked at the casket. It opened. She put out her hand and touched Tatiana's cheek. The girl opened her eyes. The mother and servants fell to their knees in fright.

"Where am I?" Tatiana asked.

They told her how the son found her and brought her to the villa. Tatiana climbed out of the casket. She told her story. They learned that she was not a doll. She never had been. She was truly a beautiful girl.

Tatiana wept with joy. "What a gift the fairies gave me," she said. "By sending me away, they saved me from my stepmother. They sealed my casket so that only love could open it. It was love that made you give up your necklace to fill the hole."

The mother was no longer afraid. She was filled with joy. "You have one more gift, dear girl," she said. "My son loves you. He will soon be here. Let us get ready for him." The mother and the servants prepared Tatiana to meet him.

Once home, the young man ran to the room with the crystal casket. He was surprised at what he saw. There was no dead girl. There was no doll. He saw a lovely woman instead.

Plans were made. The two were married. Tatiana was a wonderful wife. Those who knew her story fondly called her "the Tatiana doll."

A Roman Alphabet

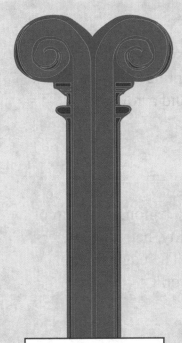

A is for *Africa*. Africa once was part of the Roman empire. It was the southern most part.

B is for *baths*. Roman men liked the public baths. The baths were like health clubs. The men played games and relaxed. They took baths, too!

C is for *Caligula*. He was a bad ruler. He thought he was a god. He wasted the riches of Rome.

D is for *Diana*. She was goddess of the moon. She ruled hunting. She often was shown with a bow and arrows.

E is for *eagle*. Every legion, or group of 6,000 men in the army, had an eagle. One man carried it. The eagles were made of gold or silver.

F is for *fishponds*. Some Roman homes had gardens. Some gardens had fishponds. People liked to rest near them.

G is for *gods* and *goddesses*. Romans had many of them. Jupiter was king of the gods. Juno was queen.

H is for *hippodrome*. It was a big sports arena. *Hippos* is the Greek word for horses. The horses pulled chariots. The people liked to watch them race.

I is for *Isis*. She was a mother goddess. Many women followed her. The Romans learned about Isis from the Egyptians.

J is for *jewels*. The Romans loved them. Some rich men and women wore a lot of rings. Rich women wore brooches, bracelets, necklaces, and earrings.

K is for *keystone*. A keystone was the last stone placed in the top of an arch. After the keystone was added, the wooden frame that held up the arch was removed.

L is for *Latin*. The people in Italy spoke Latin. People in other parts of the empire had to learn Latin, too.

M is for *makeup*. Both men and women wore it. Skin creams were made of flour and chalk. Sometimes, donkey's milk was added. Pale skin showed that a person was rich.

N is for *numbers*. The Romans used letters for numbers. *I* was one. *V* was five. *X* was 10. *L* was 50.

O is for *oxen*. Oxen were killed as gifts for the gods. They were used on farms, too. They helped harvest wheat.

P is for *port*. Ostia was the port of Rome. It was 15 miles from the city. It was on the seacoast. Corn, wine, and olive oil were kept there. The items went to market by barge.

Q is for *quadrans*. It was the smallest Roman coin. It was like our penny. Men had to pay a quadrans to enter some Roman baths. Women paid four quadrans. Children entered for free.

R is for *Rome*. Twin brothers started Rome. Their names began with *R*. Do you know who they were? (Romulus and Remus)

S is for *school*. Rich children went to school. They started when they were 7 years old. Poor children often did not go to school.

T is for *togas*. Free men wore togas. Slaves could not wear them. Plain men wore white. Senators' togas had purple trim. Emperors wore all purple.

U is for *urns*. Some urns were shaped like houses. Others looked like vases. Some had handles. They held the ashes of the dead.

V is for *Venus*. She was the goddess of love. A planet was named for her. She was shown as a beautiful woman.

W is for *wigs*. Wigs were in style in Rome. Pale hair came from German slaves. Dark hair came from women in India.

X is for *exercise*. Both men and women exercised. Men lifted weights. They wrestled. They played ball games. Women played a game called trochus. They rolled metal hoops using sticks.

Y is for *York*. York became a city in England. It was a Roman fort long ago.

Z is for *Zeugma*. It was one of the richest cities in the empire. In 2000, a dam flooded it with water. Before it was flooded, mosaics were rescued.